Religions of the World

Christianity

Ayrshire Libraries

Heinemann LIBRARY

www.heinemann.co.uk/library
Visit our website to find out more information about Heinemann Library books.

To order:
 Phone 44 (0) 1865 888066
 Send a fax to 44 (0) 1865 314091
 Visit the Heinemann Bookshop at www.heinemann.co.uk/library to browse our catalogue and order online.

First published in Great Britain by Heinemann Library, Halley Court, Jordan Hill, Oxford OX2 8EJ
a division of Reed Educational and Professional Publishing Ltd.
Heinemann is a registered trademark of Reed Educational & Professional Publishing Ltd.

OXFORD MELBOURNE AUCKLAND JOHANNESBURG BLANTYRE
GABORONE IBADAN PORTSMOUTH (NH) USA CHICAGO

© Reed Educational and Professional Publishing Ltd 2002
Sue Penney has asserted her right under the Copyright Designs and Patents Act 1988 to be identified as the Author of this work.

Designed by Ken Vail Graphic Design
Originated by Universal
Printed by Wing King Tong in Hong Kong.

ISBN 0 431 14950 X (hardback)   ISBN 0 431 14957 7 (paperback)
06 05 04 03   07 06 05 04 03
10 9 8 7 6 5 4 3 2   10 9 8 7 6 5 4 3 2 1

British Library Cataloguing in Publication Data

Penney, Sue
Christianity. – (Religions of the world)
1.Christianity – Juvenile literature
1.Title
230

Acknowledgements
The Publishers would like to thank the following for permission to reproduce copyright material:
Quotations from the Bible are taken from *The Good News Bible*, published by the Bible Society/Harper Collins Publishers Ltd, UK © American Bible Society, 1966, 1971, 1976, 1992.

The Publishers would like to thank the following for permission to reproduce photographs: Ancient Art & Architecture p. 8; C. M. Dixon p. 9; Carlos Reyes-Manzo Andes Press Agency pp. 4, 5, 7, 12, 13, 18, 19, 20, 25, 28, 30, 32, 33, 34, 40; Circa Photo Library, p. 21, 26, 31; e.t. Archive p. 10; Format p. 42; Giraudon/Bridgeman p. 17; Hutchison Library p. 39, /Nigel Howard p. 23, /B Regent p. 27; J. Allan Cash Ltd. pp. 14, 22, 29, 38, 43; Mary Evans Picture Library p. 11; Owen Franken/Corbis p. 35; Sonia Halliday Photographs p.16; The Bridgeman Art Library pp. 6, 15, 41, /M. Sconer p. 37; The Stock Market pp. 24, 26.

Cover photograph reproduced with permission of Hutchison Picture Library.

Our thanks to Philip Emmett for his comments in the preparation of this book.

Every effort has been made to contact copyright holders of any material reproduced in this book.
Any omissions will be rectified in subsequent printings if notice is given to the Publisher.

Words appearing in the text in bold, **like this**, are explained in the Glossary.

Contents

Dates: in this book, dates are followed by the letters BCE (Before Common Era) or CE (Common Era). This is instead of using BC (Before Christ) and AD (*Anno Domini*, meaning In the year of our Lord), which is a Christian system. The date numbers are the same in both systems.

Introducing Christianity

Christianity is the largest religion in the world. The people who follow it are called Christians. Christians follow the teachings of their holy book, the **Bible**, and of a man called Jesus. They believe that Jesus was the son of God.

What do Christians believe?

Christians believe in one God, who is a **spirit**. They do not believe that God is male or female. Christians often call God 'he', but this goes back to the days when men were thought to be more important than women. They sometimes talk about God as God the Father.

Christians believe that God was never born and will never die. They believe that God made everything, and sees and knows everything, too. Christianity teaches that God loves everything he made, and that he wants people to love and **worship** him.

What do Christians believe about Jesus?

Christianity teaches that the life of Jesus showed what God is like. Jesus was a man who lived in Palestine about 2000 years ago. Christians believe that he was the son of God, and that he came to earth to save people by teaching them about God.

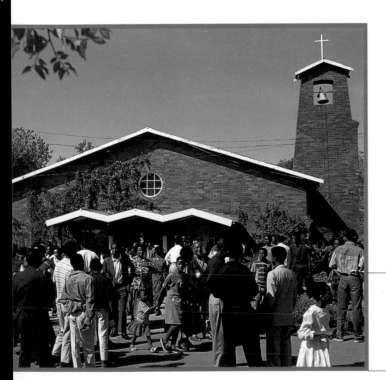

Christians meet in buildings called churches. This church is in South Africa.

Jesus is also called Jesus **Christ**. Christ was not the name of Jesus's family. It is a special title which means 'God's chosen one.'

Jesus died when he was **crucified**. Christians believe that he came back to life again after two days. This is called the **Resurrection**. They believe that Jesus is still alive today, but that he does not have a normal human body now. Christianity teaches that Jesus's Resurrection shows there is life after death. Christians teach that because Jesus died, ordinary human beings can become close to God. This means that the world will never be the same again, so they say that Jesus's death was important for all people.

▲ *The cross is an important* **symbol** *for Christians, because Jesus died on a cross.*

Facts about Christianity
- *Christianity began in the first century CE.*
- *Christians follow the teachings of a man called Jesus, who they believe was God.*
- *The most important Christian teachings are in a book called the Bible.*
- *Christians meet for worship in buildings called a church or a* **cathedral**.

The life of Jesus

*This picture of Jesus is a special painting on wood, called an **icon**. Some Christians look at icons when they **worship** God.*

Most of what we know about Jesus is in the Christians' holy book, the **Bible**. Jesus's friends and followers wanted to show why they believed he was important.

Jesus's birth

The Bible says that Jesus's mother, Mary, was told by an **angel** that she was going to have a baby. Jesus was born in a town called Bethlehem in Palestine. Shepherds were told by angels about his birth, and came to visit him. Later, wise men from a distant country came to see him. They had seen a new star in the sky and they believed this meant that an important ruler had been born.

You can find the places mentioned in this book on the map on page 44.

Jesus's death and Resurrection

We do not know much about Jesus's life until he grew up. Then he was **baptized** in a river, to show that he was getting ready to work for God. After this, he went from place to place teaching people. He chose a group of followers, called his **disciples**. Ordinary people liked listening to him. The Bible says he also worked lots of **miracles**, when he cured people of things that were wrong with them.

The people who ruled Palestine became afraid that Jesus was too popular. They decided they had to get rid of him. He was arrested, and the Roman Governor (the man who was in charge of the country) ordered that he should be killed. He was **crucified** – nailed to a cross made of wood. Then his body was placed in a cave. Everyone thought that this was the end, but two days later, some of his friends went to the cave. Men wearing shining robes told them that Jesus was alive. Then they saw Jesus himself. Jesus coming back to life is called the **Resurrection**.

During the next six weeks, Jesus's followers saw him and talked with him several times. Then an event called the **Ascension** took place, and his disciples knew that they would not see him again.

This stained-glass window shows what the Ascension might have looked like.

What happened at the Ascension?
No one will ever know what really happened. The Bible says that 'a cloud hid him from sight'. Some people say Jesus was lifted into the sky by a miracle. Other people believe he walked away up the hill into mist. Whatever happened, the disciples knew it was important. It marked the end of the time they would spend with Jesus on earth.

The early days of Christianity

Pentecost

Ten days after the **Ascension**, Jesus's **disciples** were all together in a room. It was the day of Pentecost, an important Jewish festival. The **Bible** says they heard a noise like a rushing wind, and saw flames like fire resting on each other's heads. Christians believe that this was the Holy Spirit, which Jesus had promised to send them. The Holy Spirit would help them to teach people about God.

Christianity spreads

The disciples rushed outside and began telling everyone who would listen that they believed Jesus was God's son. Then they began preaching to many people. More and more people wanted to follow the new religion. Most of the new followers were **Jews**, but some of them were not.

This caused problems, because in those days Jews did not have anything to do with people who were not Jews. How could they all share the same beliefs?

The leaders of the early Christians called a meeting in Jerusalem. Different groups put forward their point of view. One of the leaders, Peter, had been one of Jesus's closest friends. He told everyone about a dream he had had, which he believed meant that people who were not Jews should be welcomed. At last, it was agreed that people who were not Jews could become followers of Jesus too.

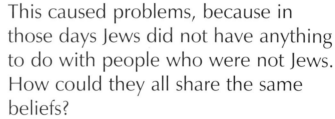

St Peter was one of Jesus's closest friends.

St Paul

One of the people who did most to spread Christianity was called St Paul. Paul had been a Jew called Saul, who had tried to stamp out Christianity. Then he had a **vision** in which Jesus had told him to stop punishing Christians. After this Saul changed completely. He changed his name to Paul, and spent the rest of his life travelling from place to place, telling people about Jesus.

▲ *Paul preached in this **amphitheatre**. It still exists in the country we call Turkey.*

What St Paul said

Paul wrote letters to Christian friends in different places. Many of his letters are found in the Bible. In his letter to friends in Corinth, Paul reminds them of things he had suffered in his life. He had been whipped and stoned, and three times the ship he was travelling on had been wrecked. Once, he had been in the water for 24 hours. He had been robbed, and had often been tired, cold and hungry. Yet, he said, everything he had been through was worthwhile, because he had been able to preach and tell people about Jesus.

How Christianity grew

▲ *This painting shows the Emperor Constantine with his mother, Helena.*

Christianity and the Romans

When Christianity was beginning, the Romans ruled much of the world. The countries they ruled were called the Roman Empire. The Romans worshipped their rulers, called Emperors. This helped to make the Roman Empire strong. The Romans did not like religions like Christianity which said that worshipping Emperors was wrong.

Some Emperors tried to stamp out Christianity. They treated Christians with great cruelty. Many were killed in horrible ways, but the Christians who died were very brave. This meant that instead of putting people off, more and more people became Christians.

The greatest change came in 313 CE. A soldier called Constantine was fighting to become Emperor. In a dream, he was told he would win the battle if he painted a Christian sign on his soldiers' shields. He did this, and won the battle. Constantine was so impressed that he made Christianity a legal religion in the Roman Empire.

Disagreements in the Church

As more people became followers, Christianity became more organized. There were meetings to sort out answers to the questions that people had begun to ask. For example, how could Jesus be God and a human being?

The leaders did not always agree on the answers. Soon the Christians divided into two groups. One group followed the leaders in Rome. The other group followed the leaders in Constantinople. In 1054 CE, these two groups quarrelled, and split apart. The Rome group became the Roman Catholic Church. The Constantinople group became the Orthodox Church.

The Reformation

For about 500 years, the Roman Catholic Church was the only Church in Europe. It was very powerful. Then some people began to question things they felt were wrong. They wanted things to change. People formed groups of their own, and began to **worship** in different ways. They were called Protestants because they had protested about the things they thought were wrong. Changes like this are often called reforms, so this time in history is called the Reformation.

▼ Martin Luther was one of the leaders of the Reformation.

Martin Luther (1483–1546)

Martin Luther lived in Germany. He felt that many of the teachings of the Roman Catholic Church were not right. He told people about his ideas and wrote books to help them understand. Many people followed him. This made him one of the leaders of the Reformation, and one of the most important men in the history of Christianity.

Different groups in Christianity

There are about 1800 million Christians in the world today. All Christians believe in God and that Jesus was the Son of God. Other beliefs are more important to some groups than to others. A group that follows the same teachings is called a Church, with a capital 'C.' There are many different Churches.

The Roman Catholic Church

About half of all Christians in the world belong to the Roman Catholic Church. The leader of this Church is called the **Pope**. He lives in a palace called the Vatican, in Rome. Roman Catholics believe that Mary was special because she was Jesus's mother. They often pray to her, and ask her to help them. They also pray to **saints** – people who were very close to God when they were alive.

Orthodox Churches

Most Orthodox Christians live in eastern Europe and Russia. Their **worship** uses lots of candles, and paintings called **icons**. Orthodox churches have a screen in the centre with icons on it. This is called the **iconostasis**. Orthodox Christians often kiss the icons and light candles in front of them. They believe this helps them to worship God.

Inside an Orthodox Church. Notice the screen with icons on it, called an iconostasis.

Anglican Churches

There are Anglican Churches all over the world. The Church of England is an Anglican Church. Anglican Churches in other countries are called 'daughter Churches' of the Church of England. They worship in ways which are very similar. The meeting for worship is called a **service**. Usually, songs called **hymns** are sung. Words which are written down in a special service book are used in worship.

Protestant Churches

Some Protestant Churches go back to the Reformation. Others are groups which have formed since that time. Some Protestant Churches are the Lutheran, Methodist and Baptist Churches. Each Church has its own way of worship. Worship usually includes reading from the **Bible**. Then a leader talks about what they have read. Ordinary people take more part in leading the worship.

A Methodist church service.

Why are there so many Churches?

Different people have different ideas. Around the world, customs and the way things are done are different. Even though Christians agree about the important teachings, they may not agree about details. Details can matter a lot when people are talking about important things like religion. Christians say that God speaks to people in different ways. The different Churches mean that every Christian can follow what they believe, in a way that is right for them.

The Bible

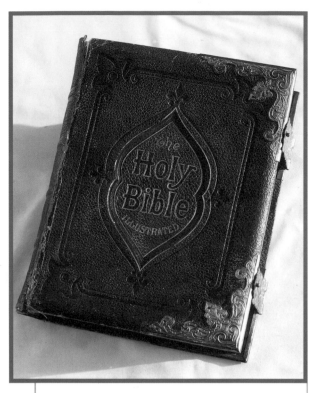

Some Bibles are very old and impressive.

The **Bible** is the Christians' holy book. It is really 66 books all collected together. The first ones were written down over 1000 years before the latest ones. The Bible is divided into two parts, the **Old Testament** and the **New Testament**. Some Bibles also include another part, which is called the **Apocrypha**.

The Old Testament

The Old Testament contains many of the holy books from Judaism, the religion of the **Jews**. Jesus was a Jew, and so were all the first Christians. The Old Testament contains 39 books. They tell the history of the Jews, and how they learned more about God. There are also story books about Jewish people, and books which contain beautiful poetry.

Why are the Gospels not the same?

The Gospels were written by different people, writing up to 50 years apart. Some may have known Jesus themselves. All of them talked to Jesus's friends. Just like you and your friends looking back on something important, their memories were not the same. They share the most important parts, but the details are different. It would be very odd if all four Gospels were exactly the same.

The New Testament

The New Testament tells the story of Jesus, and what happened after his death and **Resurrection**. The New Testament contains 27 different books.

The four **Gospels** contain most of what we know about the life of Jesus. The word Gospel means 'good news'. Christians believe that Jesus's life was good news for the world. After the Gospels is a book about the early days of Christianity. It includes a lot about the work of St Paul. St Paul wrote letters to his Christian friends in different places. When the Bible was put together, 21 of these letters were included. Christians believe the advice they contain is important for every Christian. The last book in the Bible is the Book of Revelation. Revelation means 'something shown'. It contains beautiful descriptions of a dream the writer had about life after the end of the world.

▼ *An illustration for the Book of Revelation, in a Bible produced 500 years ago.*

Stories from the Bible

The first day

God commanded, 'Let there be light' and light appeared. God was pleased with what he saw. Then he separated the light from the darkness and he named the light 'Day' and the darkness 'Night'.
(Genesis 1 v. 2)

Christians believe that the **Bible** is the most important book in the world. They believe it teaches them how they should live, and helps them to understand what God is like. The Bible contains many different sorts of teaching. The first book of the Bible is called Genesis. This means 'beginning', and it is about the beginning of the world.

The story of the beginning of the world

Genesis says that God made the world and everything in it. He did this in one week. On the first day he made light and dark. Then he made the earth and heavens, the moon and stars, the seas and everything in them. On the sixth day he made man and woman. On the seventh day he 'rested and did no work'.

Some Christians believe that this is what really happened. Others believe it is a story to help people understand how the world began. All Christians agree that the story is a way of describing the power of God.

The Resurrection

The story of the last week of Jesus's life is found in the **Gospels**. The Gospel writers believed that Jesus's death and **Resurrection** were the most important things that had happened since the beginning of the world.

Jesus died late on a Friday. The following day was the **Jewish** Sabbath, a day when all Jews have to rest. On the Sunday morning, some of Jesus's women friends went to the cave where his body had been placed. They wanted to put spices around Jesus's body, which was the custom at that time.

The Gospels say that the women found that the heavy stone which had guarded the entrance to the cave had been moved. There was no sign of Jesus's body. The women were frightened, but men wearing white robes told them that Jesus had come alive again. Some Christians believe that the men were **angels**. The women rushed to tell the other **disciples** what they had seen.

Later in the day, some of the disciples saw Jesus himself. They all became sure that he was alive again. During the next six weeks, the disciples saw Jesus several times.

This is how one artist painted the Resurrection.

Christians at home

Christians believe that God is with them all the time. They do not have to be in church to **worship**. They believe that all their lives can be part of their worship, even when they are at work or home.

Asking God to bless food before meals is called saying grace.

Prayers

Praying means talking and listening to God. Christians believe that God listens when people pray to him, and that he answers their prayers.

Not many Christians think that God speaks in a voice they can actually hear. Instead, they may receive a strong feeling, or something may happen which they believe shows them what they should do. Christians do not just ask for things when they pray. They love God, and they tell him so in their prayers.

Different Christians pray in different ways. Many Christians talk to God in the same way as they talk to their friends. They make up prayers which say exactly what they want. Some Christians also use books in which prayers are written. Some prayers have been handed down among groups of Christians for hundreds of years.

The Bible

Learning about what the **Bible** teaches is important for Christians. They read it on their own at home. Sometimes they meet in groups to study part of the Bible together.

These meetings are called Bible studies. Christians believe that reading the Bible together like this and sharing ideas helps them to understand what it is teaching.

House groups

Groups of Christians sometimes meet in each others' houses, too. This may be their only meeting for worship, or they may meet in a larger church on a Sunday as well. These Christians believe that meeting in small groups helps them get to know each other and learn more about what they all believe. They pray and sing songs together.

A group of Christians meet to study the Bible.

The Lord's Prayer

*The Lord's Prayer is the one that Jesus taught his **disciples**. It is written down in the **New Testament**. It is one of the most important prayers for all Christians. The Lord's Prayer has been translated into 2123 languages and dialects. It begins:*

Our Father, who art in heaven,
Hallowed be your name.
Your kingdom come,
Your will be done,
On Earth as it is in Heaven.

Worshipping in church

Christianity is made up of lots of different groups. Each of them **worships** in different ways. These differences are important, because it means that every Christian can worship in a way that is right for them. In most Churches, the meeting for worship is called a **service**. Services are usually held on a Sunday, which the **Bible** says is the day Jesus came alive again. Services are also held on other special days – for example, festivals like Christmas and Easter. Some Churches also celebrate **saints'** days, which remember someone who was very close to God when they were alive.

▼ *Some churches use a flat wafer for the Eucharist instead of bread.*

The Eucharist
*In most Churches, the **Eucharist** or **Holy Communion** is a very special service. The people eat a small piece of bread or a special wafer, and drink a little wine. They believe that the bread and wine become special because of the prayers that are said. They remember the last meal that Jesus ate with his disciples, and how much God loves them.*

What happens in a service?

Most services include singing special songs called **hymns**, and readings from the Bible. The readings help to show the people how they should live. There is usually a talk by the **vicar** or person leading the service. This is usually about the Bible and how it affects their lives. Some Christians use statues, candles and **icons** to help them worship.

Different ways of worship

In some Churches, worship is very quiet, and people concentrate on listening to God. The Society of Friends is a group of Christians. In their meetings for worship everyone sits in silence until someone feels that God has given him or her something to say. They feel this gives a time of peace in a very busy world. In some other Churches, worship is lively and noisy, with music and singing. Some have bands, dancing and clapping. Orthodox Churches do not use any musical instruments. The services are **chanted**, which means they are sung in a special way using very simple tunes.

▼ *A small group of Christians share a Eucharist service.*

Church buildings

The special buildings where Christians meet for **worship** are usually called churches. Some churches are large, beautiful buildings. Others are very small and simple. A church may even be an ordinary house. Some churches are very old, and have been used for worship for hundreds of years. Whatever the church is like, Christians believe that it is important because it is a place where they can meet together and worship.

This is Milan cathedral in Italy. Many people think that it is one of the most beautiful buildings in the world.

Modern churches

There are many different styles of church. Some modern churches are round so that everyone who is worshipping can see easily. Some churches now have seats that can be moved so that the rooms can be used for different purposes.

Cathedrals

The most important churches for Roman Catholic, Orthodox and Anglican Christians are called **cathedrals**. Many cathedrals are large, old buildings and are very beautiful. The people who built them did their very best work. They wanted to show how much they loved God, and how important they thought God was. A cathedral is usually where the **bishop** (a senior **priest**) is based. The name 'cathedral' comes from the proper name for the bishop's chair, which is called a cathedra.

The shape of a church

Churches are often built in the shape of a cross. This is because Jesus died on a cross. Orthodox churches are often built in the shape of a square cross (+). Sometimes they have a dome (a shape like half a ball) in the centre of the roof.

From the outside you can see that some churches have a higher part, usually at one end. If this is square it is called a tower. If it is pointed it is called a spire. All these things help to remind people to 'look up' to God.

▲ This Orthodox church is in Greece.

Many churches have bells. Many years ago, when people did not have clocks or watches, the bells used to remind them that it was time to go to church. The bells are also rung at weddings and **funerals**, and other important occasions.

Special places of worship

Christians do not believe that they have to be in a church to worship God. They can worship anywhere. However, many Christians feel that they want to go to a special place. Meeting together with other people who share the same beliefs and way of worship is also important.

Inside churches

All churches are used by Christians to **worship** God, so the things they contain are very similar. However, different groups of Christians worship in different ways, so not everything is exactly the same.

The altar

In most churches, the **altar** is the most important piece of furniture. It is a special table made of wood or stone. In some churches it is called the Communion table. It is used for the **Eucharist**, which is sometimes called **Holy Communion**. In Orthodox churches, the altar is behind the screen (the **iconostasis**) in the centre of the church.

Lectern and pulpit

The **lectern** and **pulpit** are raised platforms, usually near the front of the church. The lectern is a reading desk, used when someone reads from the **Bible**. The pulpit is used by the person giving the special talk during the **service**.

Font

The **font** is a special bowl used for holding holy water. Fonts are usually made of wood or stone. They are often very old, and may be beautifully carved. The water in a font is used in the **service** of **baptism,** when someone joins the Church.

A typical Anglican church. The lectern and the pulpit are at the front.

Other things which help worship

In some churches, the people use statues, candles and **icons** to help them worship. Stained-glass windows sometimes tell a story from the Bible in pictures. Many years ago, not many people could read or write. The stories they saw in the stained-glass windows helped them to remember the stories they heard in church.

Many churches are decorated with banners. They are often beautifully embroidered. Usually, one banner has the name of the church on it. This is used when people from the church go on processions, for example at **Pentecost**. Other banners may have the name of groups at the church – for example, Sunday School or Cubs and Brownies.

▼ *Christian symbols on an altar in a church.*

Symbols used in church

*A **symbol** is something which stands for something else. Christians use many symbols. A cross is a symbol that Jesus died. Candles are symbols of Jesus as the Light of the World. A fish is a symbol because many of Jesus's friends were fishermen.*

Places of worship

▲ *St Peter's Church in Rome is one of the most beautiful churches in the world.*

There are Christians in almost every country in the world. In different countries, the churches are often similar to other buildings in that country. This means that around the world churches are quite different.

St Peter's, Rome

St Peter's Church in Rome is one of the most splendid churches in the world. The present building was built during the sixteenth and seventeenth centuries CE. Before that, other churches had been built in the same place. This is because many people believe that it is the place where St Peter, one of Jesus's closest friends, was buried.

St Peter's Church is very richly decorated, and full of paintings and statues. It is one of the largest churches in the world. It is more than 200 metres from one end to the other – this is more than two football pitches laid end to end. It is the most important church in the Vatican. This is the palace where the **Pope** lives, and it is the centre of the Roman Catholic Church. The palace contains more than a thousand rooms. Millions of people travel from all over the world to **worship** in St Peter's, and to visit other important parts of the Vatican.

The Crystal Cathedral, California

The Crystal Cathedral in California is a very unusual church because it is built almost entirely of glass. There are more than 10,000 panes of glass in the walls and the ceiling. The idea is that having so much glass allows people to admire the beauty of God's world while they are worshipping. There are also two huge doors almost 30 metres high. They can be opened to allow an even better

▲ *The Crystal Cathedral in California is built almost entirely of glass.*

view. Many Christians believe that they can worship God through the beauty of the world they believe he made.

The Crystal Cathedral is also famous because of special **services** that are held there. The music for these services is played on a musical instrument called an organ. The organ in the Crystal Cathedral is the largest of its type in the world. It has more than 17,000 pipes!

Names of churches

*Some churches are named after a **saint**. People hope that the saint will take a special interest in the people who worship there. Other churches, especially Protestant churches, are called by a convenient name. For example, they may be named after the road on which they stand.*

Pilgrimage

A **pilgrim** is someone who makes a special journey because of their religion. Most religions have special places which pilgrims want to visit.

Why do Christians go on pilgrimages?

Some Christians believe that they will be especially close to God if they visit a particular place. Others believe it is a way of showing that they are really sorry for something they have done wrong. Sometimes pilgrims believe that a **saint** has answered a prayer. They want to go to the place which was important to that saint so they can say a special thank you. Whatever the reason, all Christians believe that their pilgrimage is part of their **worship**.

Where do Christians go on pilgrimage?

One of the most important places for Christian pilgrims is the country now called Israel. This country includes places that Jesus knew when he was alive on earth. Churches have been built where important events in Jesus's life happened. For example, there is a church in Bethlehem, where Jesus was born. For some people, these buildings are important. Many Christians like to go to the places that Jesus knew.

*A stone **altar** in the church built where Christians believe Jesus's body was buried.*

There are thousands of other places where Christians go on pilgrimage around the world. Such places may be a church where a saint is buried, or where people believe that Jesus's mother Mary or a saint appeared to people.

Some Christians believe that **miracles** can happen in these places of pilgrimage. A spring of water in Lourdes, France, marks the spot where a young girl said she had seen Mary, Jesus's mother. Some people believe that visiting this place and drinking this water cures diseases. About five million people go to Lourdes every year. Almost all of them say that their visit makes a diffeence to their life.

A pilgrim's statue

The Statue of Christ the Redeemer was built on a hill just outside Rio de Janeiro in Brazil. It shows Jesus blessing the city. It has been called one of the wonders of the modern world. Many pilgrims who go there feel that they have been blessed by seeing the statue.

Celebrating Christmas

Christmas is the time when Christians remember and celebrate the birth of Jesus. They believe that God sent Jesus to the world, and because he was born the world was changed for ever.

Advent

The four weeks before Christmas are a time when Christians look forward to Jesus coming, which is celebrated at Christmas. This time is called **Advent**. During Advent, Christians use special calendars and candles to count the days to Christmas. The calendars have doors to open or stickers to add, one for each day that passes. The candles have marks on them so that one section can be burnt each day. This helps to remind people that they are waiting for Christmas, and that it is coming closer.

Christmas

No one knows exactly when Jesus was born. Since the very early days of Christianity, people have celebrated his birth on 25 December. This date was chosen because it was already a special date. Most Orthodox Christians celebrate Christmas on 6 January, because they use a different calendar from other Churches.

These children have dressed up to perform a play about the Christmas story.

Christians usually go to church at Christmas. Special **services** are held at midnight on Christmas Eve, and on Christmas morning. Special songs called **carols** are sung. Some of them are very old. As well as carols, services include readings from the **Bible** telling the story of Jesus's birth. In many churches the story is acted out, too. Sometimes, statues of the main characters in the story are put together in a model of the scene, called a **crib**.

A Christmas crib shows the scene when Jesus was born.

Christmas customs

*The custom of giving presents at Christmas comes from the Christian belief that Jesus was God's gift to the world. Santa Claus comes from stories about St Nicholas. He was a **bishop** who lived in Turkey hundreds of years ago, and he gave gifts to poor people. Christmas trees were introduced to Britain from Germany in the mid-1800s by Prince Albert, Queen Victoria's husband. Many modern Christmas customs have very little to do with Christianity, because Christmas is a special time for many people who are not Christians.*

Celebrating Easter

Easter is both a serious time and the most joyful for Christians. It is serious because they remember Jesus dying, but it is joyful because they believe that he came back to life.

Lent

Lent is the 40 days before Easter. It is a very serious time. Christians remember how Jesus prayed about the work God wanted him to do. The day before Lent begins is called Shrove Tuesday. Shrove is an old word that means being forgiven for something you have done wrong. For some Christians this is still an important day for going to **Confession**. They tell the **priest** the things they have done wrong, and say that they are sorry. They make a fresh start for Lent.

Easter eggs

Giving eggs at Easter is a very old custom. Christians think they are like the tomb where Jesus was buried, because they look dry and 'dead' but life breaks out from inside them. Eggs can be painted or dyed in beautiful patterns. Years ago, wooden or carved eggs were given as presents. Today, chocolate eggs are the most popular.

Some Easter eggs are beautifully decorated.

Ash Wednesday

On Ash Wednesday, the first day of Lent, some Christians go to a very serious **service**. Special ash is placed on their forehead in the shape of a cross. It is a sign that they are really sorry for all the things they have done wrong.

Holy Week

During the week before Easter, which is called Holy Week, Christians remember the things that happened in the last week of Jesus's life. On Good Friday, they remember that he was **crucified**. They believe that this was 'good', because it changed the world and opened up the way to God. Special services are held in churches on this day. There are never any flowers or decorations in the church.

Two days later, Easter Sunday, is the most joyful day of the Christian year. Christians celebrate Jesus's **Resurrection**, when he came back to life. There are special services, especially during the night and in the morning. In Orthodox churches, the service begins at midnight, and the people light candles one by one so the church is filled with light.

In Orthodox Churches, Christians light candles one by one until the church is filled with light.

Celebrating Pentecost

Red and white are colours often used at Pentecost.

In many churches, **Pentecost** or Whit Sunday is a special day for being **baptized** or **confirmed**. Years ago, people who were going to be baptized wore white clothes, so the day was called White (or Whit) Sunday.

What do Christians celebrate at Pentecost?

At Pentecost, Christians remember what happened to the first **disciples** on the day of the **Jewish** festival of Pentecost. The **Bible** says that on this day all of Jesus's followers were together in one room. It was seven weeks after the Resurrection. As they were praying, they all heard a noise like a rushing wind. Then they saw what looked like flames of fire resting on each others' heads. Christians believe that this was the Holy Spirit, which Jesus had promised to send.

The Holy Spirit

The Holy Spirit is the way that Christians describe the power of God as he works in the world. They believe that the Holy Spirit is still given to Christians today. The Holy Spirit is difficult to describe, so Christians often use **symbols**. *The symbol of a dove shows that the Holy Spirit works in people in a loving and gentle way. The symbol of flames reminds them of Pentecost.*

▲ *A procession through the streets of a city in Spain to celebrate Pentecost.*

Instead of being afraid, the disciples were filled with courage. They rushed outside, and soon a large crowd gathered. The crowd thought they were drunk! Peter said they were not, and began telling the people about Jesus and what they believed about him. The Bible says that on that day 3000 people became followers of Jesus.

How do Christians celebrate Pentecost?

Many Christians think of Pentecost as the day that Christianity really began. They think that it is a day for telling other people about what they believe, just as the first disciples did. Groups from some churches join together to organize processions through their town or city. They believe that it is a good chance to share worship with other Christians. They want to show people that they believe that the Holy Spirit is still working in the world today.

Special occasions – baptism and confirmation

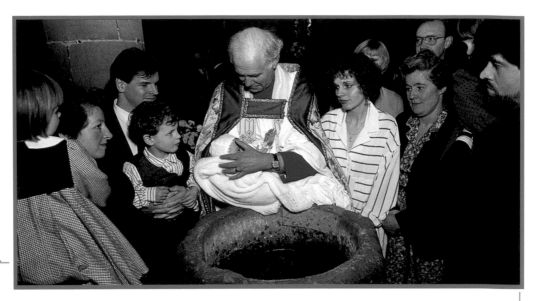

The vicar makes the sign of the cross on the baby's forehead.

Baptism

Baptism is the special service held when someone joins the Church. In most Churches, babies are baptized, but there is no age limit.

Baptism is usually part of a normal church **service**. The parents and friends of the baby's family stand near the **font**, the basin containing holy water. The **vicar** or **priest** says prayers. He or she uses a little of the water from the font to make the sign of the cross on the baby's forehead.

Gifts

*Friends and family often give a baby gifts to celebrate their baptism. These are usually things to keep and treasure. In many churches, the baby is given a candle to remind them that Jesus is the Light of the World. At confirmation, the person may be given a **Bible**.*

After this, they baptize the baby, using a special form of words. For example, if the parents had chosen the names Sarah Catherine , the vicar or priest would say: 'I baptize you, Sarah Catherine, in the name of the Father, and of the Son, and of the Holy Spirit'.

▲ *A total immersion baptism at a church in the USA.*

Total immersion baptism

In the Baptist Church, only people who are old enough to make promises for themselves are baptized. They use a special tank called a **baptistry**. The person goes down some steps into the water. They state their beliefs, and then the **minister** carefully tips them backwards so their whole body is under the water for a few seconds. This is called **total immersion**. They then leave the tank by a different set of steps, to show they are starting a new life with Jesus.

Orthodox baptism

In the Orthodox Churches, babies are baptized by total immersion, so their whole body is dipped very briefly right into the water. Then they have special oil put on eight places on their body. This is called **Chrismation**.

Confirmation

Confirmation is a service held in Churches which baptize babies. When a baby is baptized, the parents make promises for them. When the baby grows up, he or she can make those promises again, for themselves. After this service, the person becomes a full member of the Church.

Special occasions – marriage

Many Christians want to marry in church.

Marriage

Christians believe that God intended men and women to marry so that they can love and help each other. Most Christians choose to marry in church, so they can feel they are in God's house. Wherever they take place, marriage **services** have to obey the laws of the country.

The laws of most countries say that certain words must be included in a marriage service. The words must be said in front of two people, who are called witnesses. Of course, for most weddings there are far more than two people present.

The couple who are getting married are called the bride and bridegroom. During the service they make serious promises called **vows**. First they promise that they do not know any reason why they should not marry each other.

Divorce

*All Christian marriages are supposed to last for life, but sometimes this does not happen. Some Christians believe that **divorce** is wrong, but other Christians believe that it is better to allow a proper end to a marriage which has broken down. All the Churches teach that every effort should be made to mend a marriage.*

▲ *A wedding in an Orthodox Church in Greece.*

Then they promise that they will live together and love just each other until one of them dies. They may give each other special rings. The service includes songs, and prayers asking God to bless the couple. In many Churches, the service also includes the **Eucharist**.

Orthodox weddings

Weddings in Orthodox Churches are very similar, but the service is divided into two parts. In the second part, after they have given each other rings, the couple wear crowns on their heads. These may be made of silver or gold, or leaves and flowers. They are a **symbol** that God is blessing the couple. At the end of the service, they drink from the same cup, a sign of the life they will share together.

39

Death and beyond

The special **service** held when someone dies is called a **funeral**. A Christian funeral is a time of sadness but also of hope. People are sad because they loved the person who has died, and the person is no longer there. But they are also happy because they believe that death means that the person has gone to be with God.

A funeral service includes **hymns**, prayers and readings from the **Bible**. There is usually a talk about the person who has died. This celebrates the good things in their life, and remembers the sort of person they were when they were alive. There are prayers for the person who has died, and for their family and friends.

After the service, the body is either buried or **cremated**. Cremation is now more common. The body is burned at a very high temperature in a special oven. Only ashes are left. These ashes can be scattered or buried. The place where a body or ashes are buried is usually marked with a stone which gives the person's name and when they lived. The stone may also include details about their family, and anything else in their life that was important.

▼ *A funeral service in a Roman Catholic church.*

After death

Christians believe that death is not the end. They believe that the part of a person called the soul lives forever. In the future there will be a Day of Judgement, when Jesus will return. He will be a king and a judge, and will decide what should happen to everyone. This will depend on how they have lived on earth.

The Bible teaches that what happens then is quite simple. Good people will go to heaven, a place of peace and happiness. Bad people will burn forever in hell. Some Christians still believe this today. However, many Christians find it hard to believe that God, who loves everybody, would send people to burn in hell for ever. They prefer to trust God for what will happen.

▲ *An old painting showing the Day of Judgement.*

Names for death

Years ago, people were much more likely to die at a young age and in their own home. Today, people live much longer, and they are often in hospital when they die. Many people, including Christians, do not like talking about death. There are lots of ways of avoiding the word. 'Passed away', 'at rest' and 'lost' are all ways of saying that someone has died. Some Christians say that someone has 'gone to glory' to show they believe the person is with God.

Ways to be a Christian

There are millions of Christians in the world. They all believe in the most important teachings, or they would not be Christians. However, all of them are different people. They follow their religion in different ways. Some Christians go to church occasionally and try to follow Jesus in their lives. Others spend their whole lives working for their religion. Many live in a way that is between these two.

Helping other people

Christians believe that it is important to help and respect other people. They believe that God cares about everyone in the world. Some Christians show that they care about others in small ways. For example, they may visit an elderly person who lives near them, or they may do jobs for them, like shopping. In one of the stories he told to his **disciples**, Jesus said that anyone who helped somebody else was helping Jesus himself.

Some Christians spend their whole lives working with people who need help. They may work for a charity. Some charities in the UK are Oxfam, Scope and CAFOD (Catholic Fund for Overseas Development).

Caring about other people is an important part of being a Christian.

Years ago, Christians used to go to other countries to teach people about Jesus and try to persuade them to become Christians. Today, Christians who work in other countries try to help people who live there, rather than just teaching them about religion.

All Christians try to live in a way that does not harm others. For some, this means trying to look after the world, and not wasting precious things like fuel and water. It also means trying to make the world a fairer place, so that rich countries help poor countries. For others, it may mean working with groups that try to stop wars. Some Christians are pacifists, which means they believe that problems should be solved by talking, not by fighting or wars.

These nuns are working as teachers.

Monks and nuns

*Some Christians choose to spend their whole lives serving God in a special way. They become a **monk** (if they are a man) or a **nun** (if they are a woman). All monks and nuns make serious promises called **vows**. These promises mean they are able to concentrate on their **worship** and on serving other people.*

Map

The globe on the right shows the position of the map below. The map shows some important places in the history of Christianity. The ♦ symbol shows some of the places visited by St Paul.

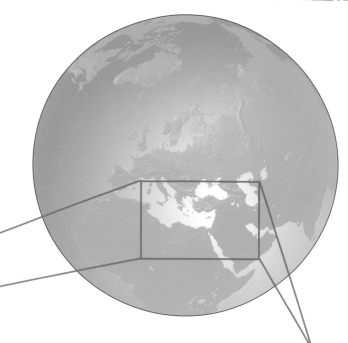

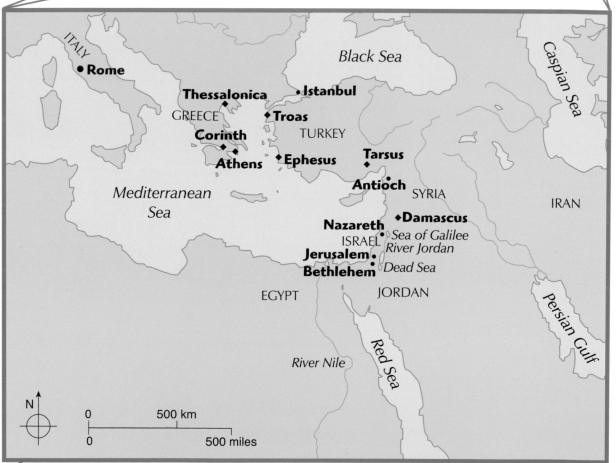

Place names

Some places on this map, or mentioned in this book are called by different names today: Istanbul was called Constantinople; Israel was called Palestine.

Timechart

Major events in World history

BCE	**3000–1700**	Indus valley civilization (Hinduism)
	c2685–1196	Egyptian civilization
	c2000	Abraham lived (Judaism)
	1800	Stonehenge completed
	c528	Siddhattha Buddha born (Buddhism)
	c450–146	Greek Empire
	200	Great Wall of China begun
	c300–300CE	Roman Empire
	c4	Jesus of Nazareth born (Christianity)
CE	**570**	Muhammad born (Islam)
	1066	Battle of Hastings and the Norman conquest of England
	1325–1521	Aztec Empire
	1400	Black Death kills one person in three in China, North Africa and Europe
	1469	Guru Nanak born (Sikhism)
	1564	William Shakespeare born
	1914–18	World War I
	1939–45	World War II
	1946	First computer invented
	1969	First moon landings
	2000	Millennium celebrations all over the world

Major events in Christian history

BCE	**c4**	Jesus of Nazareth born
CE	**c30**	Jesus of Nazareth crucified
	45	St Paul begins his Missionary Journeys
	64	Christians are persecuted under Roman Emperor Nero
	303	Massive persecution of Christians under Roman Emperor Diocletian
	313	Roman Emperor Constantine the Great becomes a Christian
	529	First monastery begun by St Benedict
	1054	The split between Eastern and Western Churches
	1483–1546	Martin Luther (leader of the Reformation)
	1525	First English Bible printed by William Tyndale
	1533	Henry VIII breaks with Rome, beginning the English Reformation
	1611	*King James Version* of the Bible printed
	1624–1691	George Fox (founder of the Society of Friends)
	1703–1791	John Wesley (the man who began the Methodist Church)
	2000	Celebrations to mark 2000 years of Christianity take place all over the world

Glossary

Advent	'coming' – the four weeks of preparation before Christmas
altar	special table used for the service of Holy Communion
angel	messenger from God
amphitheatre	area where rows of seats slope up around a stage
Apocrypha	part of the Bible used by some Christians
Ascension	event when Jesus left his disciples for the last time
baptism	ceremony in which someone joins the Church
baptistry	tank used for total immersion baptism
Bible	Christian holy book
bishop	a senior priest
cathedral	important church
chant	sing in a special way using only a few notes
Chrismation	ceremony which follows baptism in Orthodox Churches
Christ	God's chosen one
Church	a group of Christians (also the place where they meet)
Confession	telling a priest things you have done wrong, so that you can receive forgiveness
confirmation	service to confirm promises made at baptism
cremation	burning a body after death
crib	model with figures showing the scene at the birth of Jesus
crucify	kill someone by nailing them to a cross
disciple	special friend of Jesus
divorce	ending a marriage when the husband and wife are still alive
Eucharist	'thanksgiving' – an important Christian service, sometimes called Holy Communion
font	container used to hold water for baptism
funeral	service held when someone dies
Gospels	four books of the new Testament which tell of the life of Jesus
Holy Communion	*see* Eucharist

hymn	special song which people sing in services
icon	religious painting of Jesus, Mary or a saint
iconostasis	screen with icons on it
Jew	follower of the religion of Judaism
lectern	reading desk in a church
Lent	church season which comes before Easter
minister	title used for the priest in some Churches
miracle	something amazing that happens through God's power
monk	man who has dedicated his life to religion
New Testament	second part of the Bible, containing the story of Jesus
nun	woman who has dedicated her life to religion
Old Testament	first part of the Bible. It tells the story of the Jews up to the time of Jesus.
Pentecost	special day when Christians now remember how the first Christians received the power of the Holy Spirit that gave them the courage to go and preach about Jesus
persecuted	punished for what you believe
pilgrim	someone who makes a journey to a special place because of their religion
Pope	leader of the Roman Catholic Church
priest	someone set apart to lead worship
pulpit	raised platform used in church for the preacher to stand on
Resurrection	coming back to life
saint	person who was very close to God when they were alive
service	meeting for worship
spirit	being who does not have a body
symbol	something that stands for something else
total immersion	baptism where the whole body is placed under water
vicar	title used in Anglican churches for a priest
vision	dream-like religious experience
vow	solemn promise
worship	show respect and love for God

Index